ask me again

poems

hope masike

Ask Me Again

First Published in 2020
Published by Tribe Hope Foundation, Harare

www.hopemasike.co.zw
E-mail : hope.masike@gmail.com
Tel : +263 779 626 881

Edited by Memory Chirere
Cover design by Hope Masike
Typesetting by Penny Yon

ISBN : 9781-77929926-0
EAN : 9781779299260

Thirty-six poems in dedication

to Anesu Masike who was given only thirty-six years on
this earth.

to all women who live (or are trying to live) life
remembering that there isn't a spare one.

to all men who put the effort into understanding this our
world of women.

to all those searching, chiseling rocks and chasing dreams.

Contents

Foreword

Hope Masike is adventurous, determined and hardworking. She can be single-minded, forceful and demanding, all at once. Her adventurism is borne of an inbuilt curiosity to see what else is out there. Her determi-nation comes out of an inherent never-say-die spirit. And her hard work is the result of a certain impatience in seeing tangible results as quickly as possible. These qualities I have confirmed over the years, from the time back in 2012 when she, with typical determination, asked that I be a personal counsel to her. Ever since then, I have been her sounding board for all things professional and personal – mentor, if you like – who she calls "my other father".

I have watched her fascinating growth in maturity and world-view, and been amused that she still remains unsatisfied with her own develop-ment, despite being now something of a global celebrity who has even hit the World Music Charts with her most recent musical project, The Exorcism of a Spinster.

She writes songs; she sings them. She dances. She reads. She is a graphic designer. She loves fashion, stopping short of full-scale model-ling! Sometimes, once in a while, you might see her on stage, in some dramatic production. Art, in all its forms, runs through her veins. And because she is adventurous, she tries everything, which explains why she is able to fuse her mbira sounds with other musical genres with no inhibitions.

Ask Me Again is a project that has been long in the making. It marks the beginning of our discovery of yet another side of Hope Masike and the creative juices that flow within her. For me it is an extension of her song-writing skills, because song-writing in any case is some kind of poetry in itself. Who knows: out of this collection may emerge a song or two! Rather than guide your reception of it, I leave the reader to appreciate this experiment. We can only wonder what else she has up her artistic sleeve!

Ray Mawerera, Harare, January 2020

The graveyard of those who forgot to live

Here lie the nine children she never had,
She tried to hatch the eggs but they got rotten,
Over here lies the huge white wedding,
The rice, chicken, coleslaw salad and coke.
She was going to send a big bus for the entire village,
But time, true to it's very nature, ticked on,
Faster than the marriage proposal that never came.
This tombstone here reads: drive, passion and willpower,
They died together, slowly and very dramatically,
After that, she was never the same,
Withered away like harvested pumpkin leaves,
Unredeemable, she soon followed them all,
She lies here too as you can see,
Right by the entrance to the graveyard,
This graveyard of those who chased,
Then forgot to live.

Leagues of the unhappy

I don't want to join
the unhappy married women's league,
They married what their fathers accepted,
Enough coin to take care of you and yours,
The perfect dream that society sold them,
But not what they wanted.

I don't want to join
the unhappy married men's league,
They married what their mothers preferred,
Enough hips to bare, to bear children for you,
The prescription that society gave them,
But not what they wanted.

I don't want to join
the unhappy singles' league,
They married not, pleased neither parent,
Enough independence to give you freedom,
The noise of society they ignored,
But still, not what they wanted.

They are all paid for

We see mistresses of the night,
Waiting at the roadsides for the starved,
The starved then comes and pays money and money,
Then the no longer starved goes back to his real life,
Sex businesswoman? Concubine? Wife?

And another one waits on the bed for a secret lover,
So secret in their phone it's titled 'Jimmy, the plumber',
A hungry plumber comes and pays too- rent and hair and shoes,
Then, the no longer hungry plumber goes back to his real home,
Sex businesswoman? Concubine? Wife?

Yet another one waits in the kitchen for hers, a husband,
Who paid- cows and groceries and money and money,
At least she is called by his and his children's names!
Sex businesswoman? Concubine? Wife?

Just different homes,
Just different names,
And different prices.

Chairlady of the spinster association

We won't deny,
she takes very good care of herself.
Still, time cannot be deceived,
Anyone can tell she isn't sweet sixteen anymore.
Money too cannot keep a woman warm,
It's very clear that she is quite lonely.
She is way too unsmiling for a woman,
Cross her and all the sexless nights will bark at you.
She is tough, maybe she could even lead this entire kingdom

But she remains a woman,
A very aggressively bitter, slowly ageing,
lonely spinster, for that matter.
If she couldn't even find a husband,
how will she find peace for us?
We vote she remains only with her current title,
Chairlady of the spinster's association.

T for toy

It selflessly gives secret pleasures to me,
It neither kisses nor kisses and tells,
'It's also not warm, but it's you',
Eyes closed, I fantasize,
'Here, right there.'

A recipe

You can add many cups of worry,
Then watch the clock on the wall tick,
You can add big cups of hunger as well,
Then watch the mixture ferment like yeast,
Fed hunger can be a very special delicious poison,
Eyes wide shut, watch thyself become just a mistress.

Mangoes

She imagines licking the juices of the fruit
trying to escape by running down her hand,
Even if they reach the elbow, she will reach,
That is why she really loves eating mangoes,
So deliciously juicy no drop should escape.

Mother to Jezebels

If Rahab who had had only five,
You dubbed 'Rahab the prostitute',
What shall you make of me?
In your divine eyes, I am the mother to Jezebel, no?
With such filth, can I even lay under your feet to repent?
Truly, I loved every one of them, you know?
Had hoped they would make me theirs forever,
Perhaps it took me longer than all others,
To learn that none of the juice was love,
But I wonder what you then call me,
Mother to all Jezebels?

Fungayi's children

You say I can confess and be forgiven,
Many times over, I can start over again, you say,
You are way too kind,
Were I half as kind,
I'd have had Fungayi's hundredth fatherless child.

Do you then still forgive me, heathen of heathens?
Do you ever get fed up by it, confession after confession?
You are way too kind, forgiving and forgiving,
Were I half as kind,
I'd have had Fungayi's hundredth fatherless child.

Bastard

Spent an entire youthful lifetime,
Afraid of having an illegitimate child,
Bastard! Surely my mother would have buried me alive,
Now that youth is gone, smiles and life soon too,
She barks at me for a grandchild, legit or not,
She now calls me the bastard.

One bag per woman

There always is one bag per woman,
Hers, it seems seams now threaten to rip apart,
It swells and wails with red-hot fury, fury at nature,
That fresh, friendly bag it once was, is now a full, filthy junkyard,
Full of unfriendly invaders pushing even into the neighbours,
Tiring, weakening, blood-sucking evil things they are,
No space anymore for anything else.

Waiting season

I miss the mangoes' fresh sweet nourishing juice,
The tree's brand new leaves are sprouting,
Just now starting all over,
A whole full year in waiting,
If only I had dried the mangoes then!

Fields

She would have one of her own, to help her in the field,
If only seed could be picked like the soil in any field,
She would pick it, plough it up and seed her field,
If only children grew like weeds, wild in a field,
Like birds that need not work in any field.

I wish I had one

I wish I had one,
On whose head I would put a crown, hand, a sceptre,
How I would love him, put his head to rest on my soft bosom,
His hands, to heat, clenched in between my thighs,
His body, my arms and legs enveloping,
Oh how I would love him.

Purple skies and yellow clouds

Pamela woke up, a smile on her face,
She had dreamed of a world
of purple skies and yellow clouds,
Where Musengabere* was still allowed,
But for women too.

She had hired the giants Petso and Tindo,
To go grab Fatso by those long legs,
Then unseen, run away with him,
Run away with all those muscles,
All that melanin and all that smile,
And deliver him right to her sleeping mat.

*Musengabere is an ancient, 'now-dead' cultural practice where a
man who liked a certain woman and wanted to marry her was allowed
to 'kidnap' her, then send dowry later once he has her at his house.

What if

What if it had been written by women?

What if it had been a mystery, after sex who of the two shall fall pregnant?

What if it had been two books on men and sixty-four on women, all by women?

What if it had been men bleeding every month and women bleeding on the battlefields?

While justice slept

While justice slept,
They kept us away from the hearth where decisions were made,
While justice slept,
They decided that was how it had always been,
While justice slept,
They called it our culture.

Swindler

When Tendai knocks on my door,
I ask who it is,
He says. Tendai.

When I open the door,
It is Tendai,
So I let him in and we have tea.

When you knocked on my door,
The knock sounded like Tendai's,
I still asked who it was,
You said. Tendai.

I opened the door,
And you looked just like Tendai,
I let you in for tea.

You took off your coat,
And underneath it still was,
The gentle sheep I knew, Tendai,
I hang your coat and let you in more,

Let you in all the way,
Into the deep, warm cave that is my house,
Little did I know, the wolf had worn two coats.

After seeing the depths of my cave,
And smearing its walls with filthy disease,
Panting and sweating from the sweetness of my cave,

Only then did you remove your second coat,
Only then did I see it hadn't been Tendai at all,
I don't even know who this swindler I allowed in was.

Sitting pretty

So you still hope to find a virgin?
And lucky you, find one you shall!
Maybe two, maybe three, four even.
Fresh, untainted submissive innocence,
Eager, fasting to be called Mrs Anything,
Never mind all hymen raptured in your name,
The good, unaccountable, unhurried life you have!
Sitting pretty, no one exchanges your state for cattle.

The 'unsubmitting' ones

Every man in church wants to marry her,

And make their mothers glow with pride,

Every man in church wants to just play with us,

and never marry, lest their mothers die of boiling blood,

'The 'unsubmitting' ones who wear trousers, as daughters-in law?

The ones who sing in beer halls on Saturday nights, church on Sunday? No!'

Landscape

The wild curves,
The delightful casts,
The cave, for the protruding tower,
The hills here and the troughs there,
The scenic 'herscape'.

The dark hairy secrets,
They are stashed away, sacred moist,
The palatableness of a mere lick,
The sweetness of just a smile,
The warm softness of skin,
The lips that cover it.

Then the cramp,
Then the swollen feet,
Then the arching back,
Then tender breasts,
The very first home,
The nurturer.

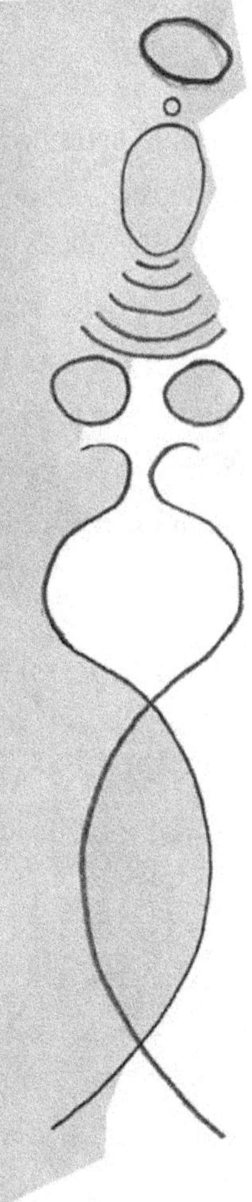

Listen

Learn to listen to the heavy silence too,
It's heavy because it is laden with messages for you,
Tongue swallow pride into silence too, so ear may hear,
There is much more to more than just your thoughts,
Tongue rest, ear listen to the fullness of silence,
Listen, how loud and honest its stories are,
It's heavy because it is pregnant
with messages for you.

Don't listen

Said enough times, soon heard,
Heard enough times, soon truth,
Truth enough soon feeds the soul,
Be wary what you lend your ears to.

Dive

A life,
Without a hurdle,
A love,
Without a thorn,
A success,
Without a pain,
Is a story
Without plot,
Dive,
Then learn to swim.

Nephew

My younger sister´s little boy,
Is a crazy and naughty nephew,
He says he wants to sleep in the girls´ room,
With his cousin Rutendo, they are great buddies,
I say look nephew, boys should not sleep in girls' rooms,
Especially when other boys are in the boys' room.
He glares at me and is lost in thought then reasons;
'Now, but you sleep in the same room with uncle?'
I explain to him that me and uncle are married,
The reasoning goes on and he barks,
'I should marry Rutendo then'.
Nephew!

Inside

Inside he can say anything,
Inside he can promise anything,
Inside he can confess everything.

Inside, where you can find the true him,
Inside, where you won't find his head,
Inside, where he is, and lost too.

Take me

Take me, possess me, control me,
Make me what you want.
Save me, protect me, cover me,
Make me what you want.
Teach me, punish me, lead me,
Make me what you want.
Own me, use me..

I love your cottage

I love your cottage,
Where only two can fit,
I love your single bed,
Where only two can fit,
I love your big heart,
Where only two can fit,
We don't need a castle,
We only need me and you.

Two pimples and a tough behind

Do you compare my small bosom to hers?

Mine are just but two pimples on a near-bare chest,

Hers are hard, perky hills that dance about as she walks,

Do you compare?

Do you compare my small, tough behind to hers?

Mine are just firm enough to sit without hurting on my bones,

Hers are wild mountains of womanhood that dance about as she walks,

Do you compare?

I hope you don't,

Because unlike her,

I was born for you, body and soul,

And two pimples and a tough behind.

It wasn't rape

Do you know how old I was back then?
Fully grown women should know better, no?
Do allow me to correct you, it wasn't rape, because I was wearing a short skirt,
And it's not as if he held an axe and forced the alcohol down my throat,
And when he started kissing me I didn't stop him; no kiss leads to prayer,
It wasn't rape because I didn't scream, I only said stop a few times,
Do you know I watched him struggle to remove my blouse,
He didn't tear it open, he took his time and I watched,
And only when he got to my bra did the alarm ring,
He is a man! Of course he was already aroused,
It wasn't rape because I left it till way too late,
It wasn't rape because when he got in,
I started enjoying, heaving, moaning,
It wasn't rape because even after,
I still spent that night with him,
It wasn't rape because after,
I kept quiet for too long,
Let me correct you,
It wasn't rape.

The Blue dress

Waking up in a pool of smelly, itchy wetness,
First thing was to hang the old, woollen blanket outside,
Then we bathed and ate purple-brown, silky porridge,
With peanut butter and pieces of bread,
And sunjam, and milk….

We were many and a half, sharing everything,
From birthdays to underwear,
And I, gotwe*, rarely got anything new,
Then the special blue dress finally came,
Special for it was one of my few, very own.

Not now though. It grew small ..., I grew bigger,
Not ever though, did my love for the blue dress change,
Please understand why I accepted the gift from him,
He remembered me, and bought me a blue dress.

*Gotwe is the last born child.

Demons and drunk hyenas

Strange,
She prays more when drunk,
More wine, more wisdom?
More wine, more eyes?
Weaker,
Vulnerable,
She sees them,
The demons, dancing,
She sees them,
The hyenas, drooling,
More wine, more danger?
More wine, more predators?
Weak prey,
Vulnerable prey,
She sees them in doubles,
Drunk, drooling hyenas,
She sees them in triples,
Dancing demons hovering above them,
Pray more soul,
They surely shall eat you,
And maybe vomit you tomorrow.

Ancestral knots

Roots tangled into a mess,
They ignored that knots shorten things,
Now we can't reach the water,
even if it floods with blessings,
They forgot that knots block,
Forgot to tend to her hair,
Now it is a messy mass,
We bear no fruit anymore.

Circles

Dark circular patches of sweat,
On your blouse, under your arms,
Dark circles under your two brown circles,
Inside two white ones, two black irises,
Circular things defining the age of your lower belly,
Two big circles on your chest, soft, warm, beautiful,
A pedant falling between your bosom, red and circular,
Big earrings hanging in circles, beaded with small circles,
Pulling your curvy ear knobs, into straight oval circles,
Your full, round circular behind, you feel it when you walk,
Up and down and side to side it gyrates in circles,
Your cuffs, knees, thighs, elbows, your life,
All circles! Just choose not the vicious ones.

Ask me again

Back then I was young,
My eyes were clouded with games and play songs,
Chihwande hwande, Champidigori, Mahumbwe and Godhabheni.

Back then you were young,
You were a sack of bones and wore urine perfume,
Soles of feet chapped, cracked skin one could write a Maths sum on.

Pardon me, I didn't see the fine heart that was hidden beneath,
Now dark skin glowing and your head is no longer too big,
And that smile, I could have never guessed.

Could you ask me again like you did when we played mum and dad?
Could we try at real love now that we are grown,
Could we? And I will say yes.

For you

For without you, how catastrophic it would be,

For I wouldn't have had anyone to share this gift with,

For you are eternally my reason why and beautifully so,

For in my words, you could find a place for space and escape,

For I appreciate you. These words I dedicate to you, yours, theirs too.

Author's Note

Sometimes I feel like *they* just have no idea, *they* just don't even know the half of it and the problem is that we think *they* know. We live with these things. We live these things. We are these things and they are so familiar to us, so much that we don't realise that, much as these things are us, *they* - *them* - have no idea.

Of course *they* are neither these things - like us - nor did *they* ever live them as we continually do. So naturally, *they* don't know these things. These things, I believe, have been so well hidden by our perhaps naively untrue and perhaps deliberately selfish interpretations of our 'culture'. And because these things stir and play with our emotions so much, when we try to tell we (maybe) use misleading tones, confusing words and emotionally-charged voices. So once again, they don't understand.

What's worse is that *they* have no idea *they* don't know. Sometimes we also have no idea that *they* don't know. When it's really worse, we are oblivious to the fact that *they* don't know that *they* don't even know. They also seem not to realise that *they* should be knowing and therefore *they* don't even know that there are these things out there, things that make us us. So it goes on and on, this not knowing.

I did these poems in a very 'open-minded' effort to find an often silent/silenced voice. There are things we do not ever say. There are things we don't know how to say. There are things that have never been said. But I agree with one poet whose work I admire - Chirikure Chirikure - who, in his introduction to his book 'Hakurarwi', said, '… and I believe that if you feel you have something to say, you must stretch out your arms to say it.' I chose to stretch out my arms and say it. I chose to write.

I may sound judgmental here and there but just remember that these things do happen! Maybe we were conditioned to never speak of them, or we were socialised to speak of them in a particular fashion. I decided to go against that and speak about these things in the most raw tone I could find inside me. My hope is to tell things *they* didn't know *they* hadn't known all along. And hopefully, make our coexistence more beautiful and less troublesome. The only blood that should shed be-tween lovers is that damn monthly menstrual flow!